DIGITAL AND INFORMATION LITERACY ™

MAKING
THE MOST OF
CROWDFUNDING

JEFF MAPUA

rosen publishing's
rosen
central®

New York

Published in 2015 by The Rosen Publishing Group, Inc.
29 East 21st Street, New York, NY 10010

Copyright © 2015 by The Rosen Publishing Group, Inc.

First Edition

Library of Congress Cataloging-in-Publication Data

Mapua, Jeff.
Making the most of crowdfunding/Jeff Mapua.—First edition.
   pages cm.—(Digital and information literacy)
Includes bibliographical references and index.
ISBN 978-1-4777-7942-2 (library bound)—ISBN 978-1-4777-7943-9 (pbk.)—
ISBN 978-1-4777-7944-6 (6-pack)
1. Crowd funding—Juvenile literature. 2. Venture capital—Juvenile literature.
3. Entrepreneurship—Juvenile literature. 4. New business enterprises—Finance—
Juvenile literature. I. Title.
HG4751.M367 2015
658.15'224—dc23

2014007514

Manufactured in Malaysia

CONTENTS

INTRODUCTION

Scott Wilson had been a director at Nike and a designer at other large companies. When Apple introduced the nano version of its incredibly popular iPod product, Wilson saw an opportunity to create something new. Rather than shoving the iPod nano into a pocket or clipping it onto a shirt, he designed a kit that would transform it into a wristwatch. Wilson took his design to Apple and other companies, hoping they would invest in the product. He was met with rejection. Undeterred, he wanted to find a way to get his idea onto store shelves everywhere. But since the traditional route of finding a corporate backer was not an option, what could he do? Wilson turned to the Internet.

The Internet age ushered in a new era of technology-based interaction. Social media made connecting with friends a virtual experience. Cheaper electronics for cameras, computers, and software lowered the price of admission into a variety of creative industries. Now just about anyone could be a filmmaker or make music from the comforts of home.

There was a shift in how websites operated. More sites got the articles and images they used for content not from employees, but from the sites' users themselves. The content creators were directly connected with the consumers. The next step saw innovators and inventors connect with people able to make their dreams come true.

The late Steve Jobs, former CEO of Apple, introduces the iPod nano. The iPod nano is a product that entrepreneur Scott Wilson would incorporate into his Kickstarter project.

A new website launched in April 2009. It allowed anyone with a creative idea to raise money to bring his or her project to life. All a person had to do was post information about it online. Anything from movies to food projects were welcome.

Traditionally, people would have to find a wealthy supporter or company willing to invest money into their project. This new website was part of a change in investing. Rather than a small number of people investing a lot of money, hundreds or even thousands of people could invest in an idea they believed in. This website was called Kickstarter. It was exactly what Scott Wilson and his watch kit idea needed.

In November 2010, Wilson attempted something new. Wilson launched TikTok+LunaTik Watch Kits for the iPod nano on the Kickstarter site. He had a modest goal of raising $15,000 in thirty days. With that money, Wilson could get the watches into production. Then something incredible happened. Within a week, the watch kit idea soared past $15,000 and raised almost $400,000. More than five thousand people saw enough promise in Wilson's idea to invest their own money in it. By the end of the original thirty-day timeframe, Wilson raised $1 million. At the time, no project had ever raised that amount of money. It propelled Wilson's company onto the global stage, and suddenly creative inventors took note of Wilson's path to success.

Funding for projects had been changed forever, and a new business and investment term was coined: crowdfunding.

Chapter 1

How It Began

Scott Wilson was part of the early years of a new wave of start-up companies. When he had an idea for a new company, the United States was in a major recession, more people were using the Internet than ever before, and profits from traditional financing were in a downward trend. Due to changes in the economy, communication, and the way people invested their money, Wilson and other new business owners had to adapt. Understanding how business and the economy changed can help explain the growing popularity of crowdfunding.

Fall of Traditional Financing

A report by National Research Council Canada focusing on companies from 1981 through 2003 revealed a shocking fact about investing in new companies. Only one in twenty start-ups were successful enough to be sold on the stock market. The news was no better for those companies that beat the odds. Only one in twenty of those initially successful companies that made it to the stock market had value for investors. In other words, investing in a start-up company was a risky decision. Even when an investor found

Traditionally, business owners would have to work with a bank to secure a loan to fund their companies.

early success, there was no guarantee that the success would be sustainable because only one in twenty returned a profit.

Investing in technology companies was a new experience for financiers. It was clear that the problem with investing in technology was speed. A computing term known as Moore's law says that computer processing speeds will double every two years. This speedy change is reflected by how fast the Internet was invented and then quickly adopted into everyday life. For investors, the speed at which technology changes affects how they invest money. Twenty years ago, investors could take their time to see how new technology performed on the market. Then they could invest in companies that showed promise. Now that investors can no longer count on new technology remaining profitable in the long term, they have to act fast if they want to make money. Think about companies like Apple or Facebook. The investors that got in at the start made a lot of money as these businesses became popular and profitable. This meant that the traditional methods of financing, which often involved looking at a company over a long period of time, had to change. Luckily, there were signs investors could look for in companies. Investors found that the best companies to invest in were the ones that could adapt and change quickly.

Traditionally, new businesses would need to buy or rent everything, from equipment to office space. One advantage of new communication technology is that employees can work from anywhere and communicate with each other over e-mail, phone, and technologies like Skype. This means that new businesses don't have to spend money on creating a physical office space. Coworkers do not even need to be in the same location. Businesses can focus investor money on developing and producing what they are going to sell to consumers. That also means they may not need as much money to get started. Traditional forms of investing, like large bank loans, might no longer be relevant for small start-ups.

Rise of the Crowd

The number of Internet users has rapidly increased over the years. The technology for the Internet has been around since the early 1960s. However, it wasn't until 1985 that the Internet was used for the purpose of making money. The number of Internet users rose from a handful of researchers at universities to include over two billion people worldwide today. That means out of every seven people, two use the Internet. Trends show that number will only go higher.

With more users online, more people are connecting with each other through different websites and web services. For example, free, open-source software is available to anyone interested in volunteering his or her programming skills. This concept, where a large group of people contributes time,

PREDICTION MARKETS

The principles of crowdsourcing can apply to predicting successful businesses. Predictions are more accurate when a large number of people share their data. Traditionally, businesses relied on experts to forecast the future of a market or industry. Business decisions were made by a select few. Additionally, they were possibly affected by personal opinions.

The strength of the crowd is sometimes called the collective IQ. This refers to the total knowledge and strengths of a group of people. This way, the strongest ideas of each person can be used. Together, the group's collective IQ is raised beyond what any one person could accomplish alone. With a large number of people, the collective IQ is even stronger and possibly more well-rounded.

In business, a company can gather the opinions of all employees to make decisions. This lowers the possibility of overlooking small details and increases potential success. Predicting outcomes, such as which product will perform well, becomes more accurate with all participants voting for their choices. These prediction markets are used in finance as well when participants select which stocks will result in profits. Prediction markets based on collective IQ can be a powerful tool.

effort, and skills into a single project, is called crowdsourcing. It has gained increasing popularity. Many of the technologies created this way power today's websites. Microsoft, one of the world's largest technology companies, dedicates a section of its website to open-source development.

As crowdsourcing becomes more accepted in the eyes of the business world, consumers take on a more active role in the market. Diners can become food critics on websites like Yelp. Television networks can no longer control what people watch on television. Sites like YouTube allow people to create their own entertainment content. Websites such as Reddit and Slashdot promote content based on what users are interested in. The general public now has influence over what people get to see. In turn, businesses have access to a large, interactive audience.

As the Internet became a staple in culture, the concept of business ownership became decentralized. That means businesses can be located in multiple locations, rather than in one place. Although this strategy is still in its early stages, there are many companies based solely online. Amazon, for example, has found incredible success by declining to build a traditional storefront in favor of an online presence.

Customers are engaged online wherever they are. A customer could post about a great restaurant right in the middle of his meal.

Peer-to-Peer Lending

After the financial crisis that began in 2008, investors and business owners began searching for investment alternatives. Peer-to-peer, or P2P, lending began in the United States in 2005 and has become a popular option. P2P works in this way: owners first determine how much money the company or project needs. They then write an explanation of the purpose of the loan for investors. Finally, they post a listing on a lending website. People who want to lend money can easily find those looking to borrow it, and their investment can be as low as $25.

P2P lending has been very successful. The top two lending sites, Lending Club and Prosper, have provided almost $4 billion in loans so far. Lenders find this an attractive option because they can earn up to 15.3 percent on their initial investment with a peer-to-peer loan. This is significantly higher than the 2.84 percent they might get from investments at a traditional bank. P2P lending has been so popular that Wells Fargo, one of the largest U.S. banks, has prohibited its employees from

Peer-to-peer lending has not made traditional banking obsolete. Instead, it has given entrepreneurs more options.

participating in peer-to-peer loans. Wells Fargo believes it is a conflict of interest and competition.

Crowdfunding

Crowdfunding came on the heels of many of these changes in the way people do business. Unlike traditional finance, crowdfunding is agile. Collective IQ and peer-to-peer lending have changed investment and how people connect to benefit a product or service. Now supporters can easily pool money and resources.

At its core, crowdfunding is about helping entrepreneurs and small business owners speak directly to the general public. This engagement then hopefully leads to financial backing. This process skips over traditional lenders like venture capitalists and angel investors (wealthy people who provide financial backing to fund a start-up company). It takes the investment opportunity directly to potential customers. This way, businesses can get an immediate idea of the type of response they will receive in the market.

Crowdfunding is a more organic, transparent way to invest. It also reflects the changes in business and general culture. Peer-to-peer lending is generally one person lending money to another. Crowdfunding is a large collection of investors cooperating on a single project.

Those who choose to take part in crowdfunding are rewarded in a variety of ways. Instead of a share of the profits, investors are treated to merchandise, exclusive access to new releases, and other perks. The rewards for investors differ from business to business. They are used to attract people to a project and encourage them to invest money. Successful projects generally have well-designed rewards that are appealing and unique.

Crowdfunding gained acceptance when the U.S. government created a law to support it as a new financing tool. Historically, small businesses were allowed to work only with investors officially recognized by the Securities and Exchange Commission (SEC). The SEC is an independent federal agency that protects investors. In April 2012, President Barack

President Barack Obama signed the Jumpstart Our Business Startups (JOBS) Act on April 5, 2012, allowing anyone to invest up to $1 million in a business.

Obama signed the JOBS Act, which allows nonaccredited, or unofficially recognized, investors to invest up to $1 million in a business. That means that anyone can become an investor at any financial level he or she feels comfortable with. This opened the door to crowdfunding in a way never seen before. Now anyone with an idea has access to financing that could make his or her dreams into reality.

Chapter 2

The Crowd Masters

rowdfunding has quickly settled in place as a usable option in the financial world. Many websites are now available to help fund businesses and projects. However, not all crowdfunding websites are created equal. They can differ in number of users and which kinds of projects they support. While one site may be good for new technology products, another may be better suited for film projects. Distinguishing one website from another is an important first step for both investors and entrepreneurs.

Kickstarter

Kickstarter is the biggest of the crowdfunding sites based on money raised. The popular website, based in Brooklyn, New York, raised approximately $100 million in funding in 2011, which rose to $480 million in 2013. Since its launch in 2009, the site has raised $1.1 billion, and more than sixty-one thousand projects have been successfully funded. Those numbers continue to rise. With a staff of less than one hundred people, Kickstarter has led the charge in crowdfunding.

Unlike other specialized sites, Kickstarter is open to any type of project. Many of the projects are creative, dealing with film, games, photography, and technology. Successful projects include Scott Wilson's iPod nano watch, the Academy Award–winning film *Inocente*, and a *Billboard* Top 10 album by musician Amanda Palmer. Kickstarter-funded art has been exhibited at several major museums, such as the Museum of Modern Art in New York City, the Smithsonian, and the Kennedy Center.

The site is open to anyone in the world. However, those campaigning for funding must be based in the United States, United Kingdom, Canada, Australia, New Zealand, or the Netherlands. Each project must be approved by staff. Once the project meets the site's guidelines and is accepted, social media and personal websites are utilized to increase

Filmmakers Sean Fine and Andrea Nix Fine, winners of the Best Documentary Short Subject award for *Inocente*, used Kickstarter to fund the project.

awareness for a project. Kickstarter provides support for fund-raisers with tracking tools and an analytics dashboard. Kickstarter only provides a platform for small businesses and entrepreneurs. It does not take a role in the development of the product. Complete control and responsibility remain with the creators.

Investors can lend as little as $1, although the minimum amount is dictated by the project's creator. These project backers are then rewarded with various gifts such as a share in the business, access to limited-edition works, free products, party and event invitations, and other perks. Backers of a book, for example, may receive a copy of the book. Those who lend more money to a project generally receive even better rewards, such as attending a film's premiere. With Kickstarter and other crowdfunding sites, choosing the right rewards can increase the chances that a project will be successful. Rewards that are boring or overpriced can hurt a campaign.

Kickstarter follows an "all-or-nothing" fund-raising model. Project creators are required to set a fund-raising goal and a deadline. If the project reaches or exceeds its goal by the deadline, then it receives all the money raised. However, if the goal is not met, money is returned to lenders and the campaign is canceled. According to Kickstarter, 44 percent of projects reach their funding goals. Kickstarter claims a fee of 5 percent once a goal is met, and there is a 3 to 5 percent processing fee. There is no fee for failed campaigns.

IndieGoGo

Conceived in 2007, IndieGoGo is another popular crowdfunding site. Its founders all failed to find funding for their own projects. Together, they sought to provide crowdfunding opportunities they did not have. The site launched in 2008 with an initial focus on finding financial backers for independent films. Its focus has since expanded.

According to its site, IndieGoGo has raised millions of dollars for thousands of projects around the world. One of those projects, from a company called access:energy, was for a way to get low-cost, clean, renewable, and

Projects such as building wind turbines to make affordable energy in low-income areas can be funded through sites such as IndieGoGo.

local energy in Kisumu, Kenya. The company's main goal was helping Kenyans build wind turbines from scratch, and it was fully funded at $25,250.

IndieGoGo's website lists the following types of projects that it funds: art, music, gaming, design, writing, technology, photography, invention, venture, green, food, political, education, community, and performing arts. IndieGoGo offers analytical tools and support for project owners and integrates with social media and individual websites for marketing and advertising. Progress is also tracked through the website.

Unlike Kickstarter, even if a campaign does not reach its goal, whatever money is raised stays with the project creator. This flexible funding plan charges a 4 percent fee if the goal is met and 9 percent if it is not. There is also an option for a fixed funding plan that charges a 4 percent fee. In cases where goals are not met in a fixed funding plan, the donations are returned to contributors.

Other Sites

There is some overlap among crowdfunding sites, giving people options for where to set up a campaign or where to invest. Kiva has been around since 2005. It has popularized crowdsourced microlending. Microlending is the

File   Edit   View   Favorites   Tools   Help

FAILED PROJECTS

FAILED PROJECTS

A downside of crowdfunding is fraudulent or fake campaigns that have no intention of following through on their claims. Even entrepreneurs with the best intentions can create a failed product. Project backers are at risk of losing their investment when a company takes the funds and disappears.

ZionEyez, later renamed Zeyez, is one of the most famous failed projects. The company claimed to be developing glasses that had a built-in camera and microphone. The glasses would record high-definition audio and video, then have the ability to post it on the Internet immediately. The company created a Kickstarter campaign and set a goal of $55,000. When the campaign closed on July 31, 2011, the company had raised a total of $343,415 from 2,106 backers. The plan was to have a working product by the end of the year.

By winter of 2011, there was no sign of working glasses. Zeyez sent a prototype to a technology review website but reported that there was still much work to be done. It was looking like Zeyez would not be able to sell the glasses to the general public by the original deadline of July 31, 2012. The backers of the product were not pleased. Further frustrating them was the lack of communication from the company. By January 2014, the company had not released a working model, and the project backers lost their investments.

While Kickstarter and other crowdfunding sites have basic controls in place to prevent dishonest funding campaigns, they warn potential investors to carefully review projects before committing money. According to Kickstarter, of its more than one hundred thousand (and rising) projects, less than a dozen have been closed due to fraud concerns. While the users can alert the site to questionable projects, there is no guarantee of success for even non-fraudulent campaigns. The backers of Zeyez had to learn this lesson by experience.

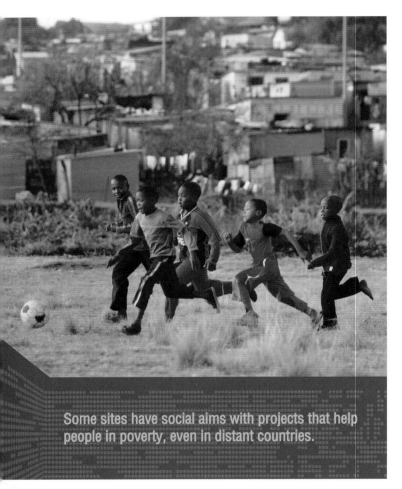

Some sites have social aims with projects that help people in poverty, even in distant countries.

practice of making very small loans to people who do not have access to traditional banking systems. The most common loan on Kiva is $25. Kiva made it possible for entrepreneurs around the world to get funding for their businesses, with the end goal of helping to decrease poverty. The site claims to have made nearly $524 million in loans from over a million lenders.

Unlike Kickstarter and IndieGoGo, Kiva requires business owners to repay their loans over time. Kiva is a nonprofit organization. Therefore, it does not take a fee from loans. According to Kiva, nearly 99 percent of loans are repaid.

RocketHub, launched in 2010, is open to all types of projects. Most of its campaigns, however, are aimed toward social goals such as teaching children to ride bikes or fighting homelessness. Even the science-based campaigns have social aims. Studying animal behavior, preventing disability in rural areas of third-world countries, and teaching about climate change are a few. Special opportunities are offered through the site, such as working with a publicist to help promote a project or creating opportunities for artists to exhibit in a museum. RocketHub does not charge fees. Any money raised is kept by the project owner.

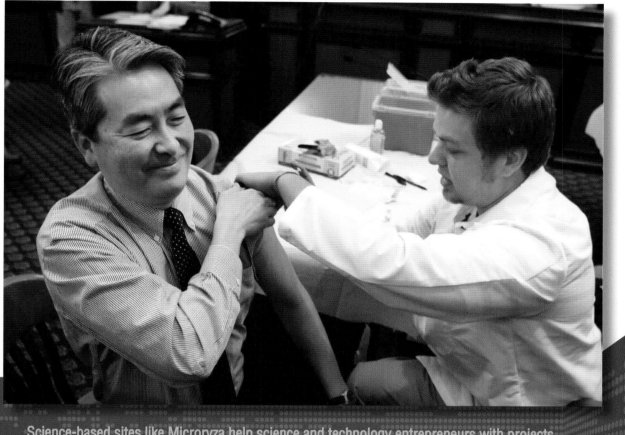

Science-based sites like Microryza help science and technology entrepreneurs with projects such as creating better vaccines.

Launched in 2012 by a group in Seattle, Washington, Microryza funds science- and technology-based projects. Many highlight academic works and seek to expand scientific knowledge. The site's goal is to connect scientists and researchers with people interested in funding their projects. Some projects include learning about global warming, saving species from extinction, or producing better flu vaccines. Microryza follows the all-or-nothing funding model. It charges a 10 percent fee on successful campaigns.

TEN GREAT QUESTIONS

TO ASK A CROWDFUNDING EXPERT

1. Why would you choose to crowd-fund a project over finding traditional funding?

2. How do you handle marketing your project and letting people know about it?

3. What are the best ways to communicate with lenders and potential lenders?

4. How do you manage and maintain a campaign as it is happening?

5. What kinds of things are you looking for when choosing a project to fund?

6. How did you put your campaign together?

7. How did you decide on the amount to invest?

8. What lessons did you take away from your last campaign or investment?

9. What would you do differently if you had to fund your project again?

10. After the campaign was over, how did you maintain contact with investors or the project owners?

Chapter 3

Making Crowdfunding Work

rowdfunding grew from an investing alternative to a full-blown industry. Multiple companies now compete to offer services to small businesses and entrepreneurs. Crowdfunding helps people chase their dreams. Friends and family can support their loved ones. But how does it work, and is it an option for everybody? How does someone prepare for a fund-raising campaign?

Who Should Crowdfund?

Jan Jensen, an experienced Kickstarter fund-raiser, said of crowdfunding, "If you think crowdfunding is easy, guess again: It's definitely not. It's the Internet and you have to expect mixed feedback."

Fund-raisers can't get discouraged easily. Project creators must be confident in their idea or product. The first thing they must honestly ask themselves is how good their idea really is. Anyone crowdfunding a project must know what value his or her product or service provides, as well as what makes it different from competitors.

Communication itself can be tricky. Rather than presenting to traditional investors, project creators speak directly to consumers. These potential investors have a wide range of backgrounds and cultures. Crowdfunding project owners must be able to express their ideas while also getting people excited about the product or service. A campaign needs someone who understands the target audience and can speak to potential backers.

Project creators must also be sure they can fulfill their promises to backers. When people invest their money in a business, they expect deadlines and goals to be met. Failed campaigns, such as the Zeyez project, have had major negative impacts on the campaign managers. Failures can also affect funding for future projects. Additionally, along with success come higher expectations. Projects receiving large funds will need to outperform the competition. Project creators must be ready to go beyond original goals.

Crowdfunding is not an option for everyone. People tend to respond more positively to smaller companies or individuals than large companies or wealthy people. Actor Zach Braff came under fire in 2013 when he launched a Kickstarter campaign to fund his movie. Many thought Braff

Crowdfunding also leaves project creators open to public criticism, as in the case of Zach Braff and his movie project.

File   Edit   View   Favorites   Tools   Help

PROS AND CONS OF CROWDFUNDING

PROS AND CONS OF CROWDFUNDING

There are many benefits and disadvantages to crowdfunding a project. Deciding if crowdfunding is the right option can depend on the importance of each of these points.

Crowdfunding allows creators to control everything about their project. They control costs, delivery, execution, and customer communication. No one but the creator owns the project or business. However, this also means that there will be a good amount of stress. Running a campaign is hard, and there are unexpected problems even in successful projects.

Crowdfunding provides a good way to test a product's popularity, or "pre-sell." The public can view a prototype and give immediate feedback, allowing the creator to fix problems. Project backers help promote the campaign and increase the number of people who see the invention. But getting ideas in front of the public can backfire. People can be brutally honest in their opinions. Also, competitors will have the opportunity to evaluate a campaign and base their decisions off of someone else's work.

Although not common, some projects are given much more money than they need. Traditional investing sometimes takes multiple rounds of funding to reach a goal. Crowdfunding can provide all the money a company needs in one round. However, it does not always work. Especially with the "all-or-nothing" funding model used by Kickstarter, entrepreneurs may not see any money at all if their goals are not met. Project creators are encouraged to have a backup plan should crowdfunding fail.

was taking advantage of the crowdfunding model since he had access to traditional fund-raising as well as his own money. Public opinion turned on Braff, who had to respond to numerous questions about his motivations, as well as charges that he was not appropriately rewarding his backers.

Prelaunch Research

A project can exceed its goals and raise two, three, or even up to sixty-six times the original goal, as with Scott Wilson's TikTok+LunaTik Kickstarter campaign. However, this kind of success does not happen without a lot of prior work. Project creators must have something to help potential backers visualize the final product. The financial goal, including how much money

One surprisingly well-backed Kickstarter was the *Reading Rainbow* project launched in June 2014. Many young people contributed to restarting a show that they watched when they were kids.

it will take to complete a project and how much taxes and rewards cost, must be calculated. Budgets should allow for breathing room in case there are surprise costs.

Once the budget, goals, and deadlines are calculated, project owners must decide on a crowdfunding platform. Some people choose to use sites like Kickstarter and IndieGoGo, while others choose to create a new website themselves. A mixture of both is also an option.

Researching and learning about what made previous campaigns succeed or fail is an important step. Research includes looking closely at the interest level of a product, service, or event. Is the project clearly explained and targeted to the appropriate audience? Project creators should look at a competitor's promotional video to see if it was produced well and communicated important information. Which of the competitors' rewards get good responses from backers? Finally, how do other campaigns market themselves and interact with potential lenders? Is there good communication? Why do fans rally behind the project or turn against it?

The Pitch

Potential backers' first encounter with a project is its pitch. The pitch is done via video. It should clearly and briefly explain the project and its value. Videos need to capture someone's attention in the first few seconds. But most of all, video pitches must be convincing.

Creating the perfect pitch requires knowledge of marketing, social networking, and how to gain customers. It is helpful to practice in front of friends and potential customers. This will help identify where the pitch is strong and where it can be improved. Any positive material related to a project should be used. A pitch can include concept art, prototypes, working scenes in a movie, or parts of a song. Notes of support from notable individuals can also help strengthen a pitch. These materials will define a project and help promote it over the course of a campaign.

A project video helps attract potential investors. It does not have to be made professionally, but it should be clear and interesting.

Note that a pitch should be reasonable and not promise something that cannot be done. Stretch goals are goals that are introduced after reaching the original goal. They can be used for riskier updates further down the line.

Rewards

Since crowdfunding does not normally provide investors with a part of the business's profits, they must be rewarded in other ways. Project

Investors can be rewarded for their support with such benefits as free samples, their name on the product, or other offerings.

creators must decide what they can offer and at what cost. Those who contribute more expect to receive better rewards for their money. Luckily for project creators, there are many options for fun, unique, and memorable rewards.

One barn-building project rewarded lenders by naming goats after them. An ice–cream parlor offered to name flavors after its backers. A musician listed supporters as performers in the credits, and one filmmaker even tattooed lenders' names onto his arm. Interesting rewards can help promote a project in a way normal media cannot.

In addition to becoming the first investors in a project, friends and family can provide valuable feedback about what could appeal to them and potential investors.

Early Start

With everything in place, project creators should get an early start by getting friends and family interested. This can create a strong start to a campaign. If there is an existing group of supporters or fans, they should be engaged right away, too. This can be done by asking for their opinions about the project and possible rewards. Video game developer Brian Fargo practiced this with his *Wasteland 2* project, and it helped launch the project on a positive note.

MYTHS & FACTS

MYTH Crowdfunding is online panhandling and begging.

FACT Crowdfunding is a way to support a project or an idea, not a single person. It is more than just raising money; it is building an audience to get behind a product or cause. People become participants in a project and help bring a creative idea to life. The shared enthusiasm for a project gets a community involved.

MYTH Crowdfunding is only about the money.

FACT Launching a campaign can help raise awareness about a creative project and market it beyond someone's immediate circle. A project can also provide feedback about an idea and allow the market to assign its value. Entrepreneurs can also connect with collaborators and business partners, which can open new opportunities.

MYTH A big social following is necessary for success.

FACT Social media is only one tool to connect with an audience. A person's immediate circle can contribute a large amount and can also begin the promotional phase of a campaign. However, more personal contact, such as phone calls or personal e-mails, is a more effective way of reaching out to potential lenders.

Chapter 4

Ready, Set, Go

The research is complete, the rewards are set, and the pitch is perfect. The budget has been properly calculated, and a deadline has been chosen. All resources have been gathered and are ready for use. Now what? Project creators have to identify their target audience and learn how to reach those individuals. Marketing and advertising are important for success, but how are crowdfunded projects promoted? How should an entrepreneur interact with the general public?

Starting the Clock

Something to take into consideration is when to launch a campaign. Brian Fargo, maker of the video game *Wasteland 2*, noted, "One big mistake we made was launching on a Tuesday at 5 AM. When you launch determines when your project ends. We could also have promoted that last opportunity to pledge [in] those final hours. But not on a Tuesday at 5 AM." Plan properly because once a campaign begins, there is no turning back.

It is important for a project to get off to a good start. That includes how and when the project is launched.

Project creators should contact friends and family before launch to make sure the campaign starts quickly. Many people on sites like Kickstarter keep a blog to update anyone interested in the project. This opens a line of communication to the general public and can be a way to show people the work being done. Another trick that people use is slowly revealing the rewards. Doing so helps keep up interest levels, and revealing them on a set schedule creates a regular rhythm for the campaign. People will be well informed about when to come back for more updates on the project.

Communicating

For successful projects, expect that there will be a lot of communication with backers. Brian Fargo said that his public-relations in-box would receive

Communication is key to a successful project. Potential investors may have questions or concerns that should be addressed promptly. It can be easy for project organizers to become overwhelmed.

fifteen hundred e-mails with questions ranging from media requests to problems with credit cards. The sheer number of e-mails was intimidating. Many people with crowdfunding experience note how important it is to continuously communicate with backers.

People donating money need to see that their money is not being wasted. In addition to answering e-mails, project owners should use online forums to stay in contact and release mass updates to everyone. The goal is to keep people talking and nurture excitement about a project.

Marketing and Advertising

There are two parts to marketing and advertising. The first is calling attention to a product. The second is promoting and selling it. After a project is launched, the most important task for a project owner is to create buzz. That means maintaining an atmosphere of excitement around the project. This will make the campaign grow bigger and bring in more money.

Crowdfunding requires project owners to use marketing and advertising skills like large corporations. Creating a brand can be just as important for a small project as a big one.

File   Edit   View   Favorites   Tools   Help

SOCIAL HELP

SOCIAL HELP

Social media sites like Facebook and Twitter are great ways to promote a campaign. There are a large number of sites available today, so creating a formal strategy and checklist is a good way to keep organized. Maintaining hourly, daily, and weekly tasks makes it easier to understand and effectively use social media.

Many campaigns create Facebook pages and Twitter accounts. People can "like," "subscribe," or "follow" these accounts and receive updates as they happen. Although they are both powerful tools, they are not the best way to gain loyal fans and potential backers. Instead, they should be used in addition to joining established communities and organizations. Other social media sites such as LinkedIn and Reddit can also be very useful. Each has its own set of rules that should be followed.

The key to social media is having popular and influential fans and followers. It takes time and effort to create a network, but the effects can be incredible.

It means constantly updating the campaign information, calling potential lenders, handing out promotional material, and using social media such as Twitter and Facebook.

The marketing and advertising industry relies on many different types of knowledge. Marketing and advertising professionals understand art and behavioral science. It is unlikely a project creator can master all the skills of a professional. Instead, it is more beneficial to understand the types of marketing. Brand marketing focuses on letting people know what a product is about and raising awareness. Direct marketing, such as a sign that says

"50 percent off sale today," addresses specific wants and needs. Making use of both types, rather than just one, will help strengthen a campaign.

Many project owners cannot handle the amount of marketing and advertising needed. Luckily, there are many tools available. Many applications and computer programs allow businesses to send messages to multiple social media sites at once. Industry events and conventions are also helpful for raising awareness. This is particularly successful with people who are already familiar with the specific product a campaign sells. At these conventions, promotional materials can be handed out, and people can talk about the campaign in person.

There are public relations companies that help with the marketing and advertising branch of a business. They can help a business get in contact with journalists and other media members who will then write about or promote the campaign to their readers or fans. Good public relations companies have connections to people that are not available to the general public. They handle social media sites, such as Facebook and Twitter, and help spread word about the campaign.

Note that traditional advertising, like commercials and paid advertisements, have not been popular with crowdfunding campaigns. Social media and positive press coverage have proven to be more effective.

Campaign Completion

Once the deadline is reached and the campaign is closed, there are a few steps left to ensure success not only for the current project but future ones, too. All backers must be thanked, to promote gratitude and trust. They deserve to have their enthusiasm for a project returned by its owner. Rewards must be sent out as soon as possible, and lenders' contact information needs to be collected.

Project owners should stay in touch with their backers. Many campaigns keep a blog that anyone can read to see what updates are being made and how the project is coming along. An added benefit is possibly

The end of a crowdfunding project means a new focus. A successful project has to meet promises to backers. An unsuccessful project will have to be rethought and started again.

gaining more fans who will then turn into paying customers once the project is available to the general public. These update blogs should be run on websites separate from the crowdfunding sites.

One thing that most people do not consider is tax responsibility. Crowdfunding experts recommend contacting a professional financial adviser such as a certified public accountant to determine the amount of taxes owed on crowdfunded contributions.

For campaigns that do not reach their goals, project creators should not be too discouraged. Realistically, not every project will reach its goal. The recommendation is to improve on the plan and presentation and try again. With better research and an adjusted target audience, a second try may find success.

Crowdfunding is a powerful tool available to anyone. Where it was difficult before to find a wealthy benefactor for an idea, the Internet has opened the doors to any hopeful entrepreneur. With hard work, preparation, and a little bit of luck, any great idea can become a reality.

GLOSSARY

advertising Calling public attention to a product or service.

buzz An atmosphere of excitement and activity.

campaign Organized and active work toward a particular goal, such as raising funds.

crowdfunding The practice of funding a business or a project by a large number of people.

crowdsourcing The practice of assigning tasks to a large number of volunteers.

decentralized Located in multiple locations rather than in a single center.

entrepreneur A person who organizes and operates a business while taking on financial risks to do so.

innovator A person who devises new ideas for products or methods.

marketing Promoting and selling products or services.

microlending The practice of making very small loans to people who do not have access to traditional banking systems.

open source Computer software for which the source code is free to all.

pitch Promotion of a campaign by means of making an argument for and demonstration of a new product or service.

profit The amount of money gained after subtracting operational costs from total income.

start-up company A business or organization that has just begun and is in the early stages of operation.

venture capitalist A person who invests funds into a new or unproven business.

Canadian Institute of Entrepreneurship
http://www.cieasia.org
The Canadian Institute of Entrepreneurship, which is run entirely online,
    provides business education for thousands of business students and
    entrepreneurs.

Canadian Youth Business Foundation
133 Richmond Street West, Suite 700
Toronto, ON M5H 2L3
Canada
(866) 646-2922
Website: http://www.cybf.ca
The Canadian Youth Business Foundation offers entrepreneurs services that
    are built around the "life cycle" of a young entrepreneur, helping to
    ensure the success of every new start-up.

Consortium for Entrepreneurship Education
1601 W Fifth Avenue, #199
Columbus, OH 13212
(614) 486-6538
Website: http://www.entre-ed.org
The consortium develops entrepreneurship education on the philosophy that
    entrepreneurship education is a lifelong learning process.

DECA Inc.
1908 Association Drive
Reston, VA 20191
(703) 860-5000
Website: http://www.deca.org

DECA prepares students in high schools and colleges around the globe who are interested in careers as entrepreneurs in marketing, finance, hospitality, and management.

Junior Achievement
One Education Way
Colorado Springs, CO 80906
(719) 540-8000
Website: http://www.ja.org
Junior Achievement is the world's largest organization dedicated to educating students about workforce readiness, entrepreneurship, and the economics of life through hands-on programs.

National Federation of Independent Business (NFIB)
    Young Entrepreneur Foundation
53 Century Boulevard
Nashville, TN 37214
(800) 634-2669
Website: http://www.nfib.com/foundations/yef
The NFIB Young Entrepreneur Foundation educates and helps students interested in small business and entrepreneurship further their education.

Websites

Because of the changing nature of Internet links, Rosen Publishing has developed an online list of websites related to the subject of this book. This site is updated regularly. Please use this link to access this list:

http://www.rosenlinks.com/DIL/Crowd

FOR FURTHER READING

Bateman, Katherine R. *The Young Investor: Projects and Activities for Making Your Money Grow.* Chicago, IL: Chicago Review Press, 2013.

Bryant, Jill. *Phenomenal Female Entrepreneurs.* Toronto, ON: Second Story, 2013.

Crilley, Dallas. *Kidpreneur Genius Way for Kids to Pay Their Way Through College!* Dallas, TX: Brown Books, 2008.

Gagne, Tammy. *Investment Options for Teens.* Newark, DE: Mitchell Lane Publishers, 2013.

Hill, Napoleon, Joe Flood, and Cullen Bunn. *Think & Grow Rich from SmarterComics.* San Jose, CA: Smarter Comics LLC, 2012.

Kamberg, Mary-Lane. *How Business Decisions Are Made* (Real World Economics). New York, NY: Rosen Publishing, 2012.

Karlitz, Gail, and Debbie Honig. *Growing Money: A Complete Investing Guide for Kids.* New York, NY: Price Stern Sloan, 2010.

Neiss, Sherwood, Jason W. Best, and Zak Cassady-Dorion. *Crowdfund Investing for Dummies.* Hoboken, NJ: Wiley, 2013.

Rankin, Kenrya. *Start It Up: The Complete Teen Business Guide to Turning Your Passions into Pay.* San Francisco, CA: Zest, 2011.

Steinberg, Don. *The Kickstarter Handbook: Real-Life Crowdfunding Success Stories.* Philadelphia, PA: Quirk, 2012.

Sutherland, Adam. *Start Your Own Business* (Quick Experts Guide). New York, NY: Rosen Publishing, 2014.

Wilkinson, Colin, *Growing Your Digital Business: Expanding Your Social Web* (Digital Entrepreneurship in the Age of Apps, the Web, and Mobile Devices). New York, NY: Rosen Publishing, 2013.

Williams, Gabrielle J. *The Making of a Young Entrepreneur: A Kid's Guide to Developing the Mind-Set for Success.* South Bend, IN: Legacy Builder Group, LLC, 2011.

BIBLIOGRAPHY

Alloway, Tracy, and Arash Massoudi. "Wells Fargo Bans Staff from Investing in P2P Loans." CNBC.com, January 21, 2014. Retrieved January 2014 (http://www.cnbc.com/id/101350320).

Chhatbar, Arvind, ed. *Converging Technologies and New Product Markets, Roundtable VIII Report. 8th ed.* Ottawa, ON: National Research Council of Canada, 2003.

Child, Ben. "Zach Braff Kickstarter Controversy Deepens After Financier Bolsters Budget." *Guardian*, May 16, 2013. Retrieved February 2014 (http://www.theguardian.com/film/2013/may/16/zach-braff-kickstarter-controversy-deepens).

Gibbs, Mark. "The Truth About Kickstarter and ZionEyez." *Forbes*, August 20, 2012. Retrieved January 2014 (http://www.forbes.com/sites/markgibbs/2012/08/20/the-truth-about-kickstarter-and-zioneyez).

Indiegogo.com. "About Us." Retrieved January 2014 (http://www.indiegogo.com/about/our-story).

Indiegogo.com. "Ten Myths of Crowdfunding." Retrieved January 2014 (http://landing.indiegogo.com/10-myths-of-crowdfunding).

Kickstarter.com. "What Is Kickstarter—Kickstarter." Retrieved January 2014 (https://www.kickstarter.com/hello?ref=nav).

Kiva.org. "About Us." Retrieved January 2014 (http://www.kiva.org/about).

Lawton, Kevin, and Dan Marom. *The Crowdfunding Revolution: Social Networking Meets Venture Financing.* Seattle, WA: CreateSpace Independent Publishing Platform, 2010.

Pinchefsky, Carol. "10 of the Most Clever Kickstarter Rewards." *Forbes*, January 23, 2013. Retrieved February 2014 (http://www.forbes.com/sites/carolpinchefsky/2013/01/23/10-mos-clever-kickstarter-rewards).

Rusli, Evelyn M. "Kickstarter Project Canceled Amid Fraud Accusations." *Wall Street Journal*, November 12, 2013. Retrieved January 2014 (http://blogs.wsj.com/digits/2013/11/12/kickstarter-project -canceled-amid-fraud-accusations).

Steinberg, Scott, and Rusel DeMaria. *The Crowdfunding Bible: How to Raise Money for Any Startup, Video Game, or Project*. Read.me, 2012.

U.S. Small Business Administration. "P2P Lending and Crowdfunding—Explore the New Frontier for Small Business Lending." May 29, 2012. Retrieved January 2014 (http://www.sba.gov/community/blogs/p2p-lending -and-crowdfunding-%E2%80%93-explore-new-frontier-small-business -lending).

Young, Thomas Elliott. *The Everything Guide to Crowdfunding: Learn How to Use Social Media for Small-Business Funding*. Avon, MA: Adams Media, 2013.

INDEX

About the Author

Jeff Mapua is a graduate of the University of Texas at Austin with a focus on mathematics and finance. As a writer and editor for over ten years, he writes for students of all ages and has written teachers' guides to help them connect with their students. His work has appeared in magazines, books, and on several websites. Mr. Mapua lives in Dallas, Texas, with his wife, Ruby.

Photo Credits